Lichen Songs

New and Selected Poems

George Venn

This book is for
Alice, Judy, Ann, Barbara, Carol, Donna,
Elizabeth, Elaine, Jo, Jean, Katherine, Marie, Mandy, Marolane,
Sarah, Sharon, Stephani, Vernita, Vi–all love's alphabet

Selected Works by George Venn

Poetry
West of Paradise: New Poems
Marking the Magic Circle (with photographer Jan Boles)
Off the Main Road (with artist Don Gray)
Sunday Afternoon: Grande Ronde (with artist Ian Gatley)

Non Fiction
Beaver's Fire: A Regional Portfolio (1970-2010)
Keeping the Swarm: New and Selected Essays
Darkroom Soldier: Photographs and Letters from the South Pacific Theater World War II. With Fred H. Hill
Soldier to Advocate: C. E. S. Wood's 1877 Legacy

Works Edited
Fred Hill: A Photographer's Life
The *Oregon Literature Series*, Vols. 1-6
Amelia Diaz Ettinger, *Speaking at a Time* (poems/translations).
Lars Nordstrom, *Ten New Lives: Swedes in the Pacific Northwest*

Acknowledgments
Special thanks to Stephani Stephenson, John Witte, and Paulann Petersen for their stellar assistance in shaping this collection.

Cover by Jan Boles: "Lichen on Purple Sage." Sunny Slope, 2/6/10. www.janboles.com

Author photo by Stephani Stephenson: www.revivaltileworks.com.

This page cannot legibly contain all copyright notices and acknowledgments. Pages 124-125 constitute an extension of this copyright page.

ISBN 13: 978-1-947465-03-9

CONTENTS

from OFF THE MAIN ROAD (1978)

Fall Dance	8
Tomato	9
Setting Backfire	10
Words	12
Song for Carpenters After Summer	13
Poem Against the First Grade	14
Directions for Visitors	16
Bird Talk	18
Split Kindling	19
Forgive Us...	20
Inviting Alex to the Bees	22
Report on Grandparents' House	23
How to Live Two Days in Osburn, Idaho	24
Off the Main Road	26

from MARKING THE MAGIC CIRCLE (1987)

Early Morning: Washington 12 toward Ohanapecosh	28
My Mother Is This White Wind Cleaning	30
High Cascades	32
Larch in Fall	33
The Black Wolf of Love	34
A Gallon of Honey in Glass	36
Conjuring a Basque Ghost	37
Report from East of the Mountains	38
Coyote Teaches Jesus a New Word	40
Professors in Their Masks as Fence Posts	41
Blue Hour: Grandview Cemetery	42
Sleeping Upstairs	44

from WEST OF PARADISE (1999)

The Emperor Breeds Only on the Ice	46
Five Six Minutes in March	48
Among Decoys	50

In the Time of Gold Trees	52
Excuses in Snow	53
A Hanford Veteran: Jay Mullen's Story	54
On West Burnside, Portland	56
Gyppo	57
A. J. Dickey Couldn't Run the Ends	58
Segues for Interstate 84, Westbound	60
Fable for an Arrogant Century	65
A Father Speaks to His Son the Only Boy in the Seventh Grade Choir	66
Voice from Another Wilderness	67
Family Scavenger	68
The Treehouse at 316 North Regent Street, Burlington, Washington	70
My Aunt, Helen of Avon	72
Uncle Leonard, Penitent	74
Elegy for a Migratory Beekeeper	76
Grandma Wilhelmina at Eighty-Five	78
Star	80
The Lichen Family Story	81
June Night, Full Moon	82
Eagle Cap	83
Water Music, The Upper Imnaha River	84
A Dream of Two	86

from PUBLISHED UNCOLLECTED POEMS (2000–)

In the Cabinet Shop, You Never Know...	88
Awakening	90
Blue Mountain March	91
Crawl Space	92
Easter on "B" Avenue with Doe and Fawns	93
Street Cries, Spain	94
The Engineer in Love at Fifty-Five	96
Spring Work	98
Teacher in the Desert	99
The World According to Apples	100

from NEW AND UNPUBLISHED POEMS (2000–)

Inside the Foreign Experts' Compound	102
After Divorce	103
Waiting for the Bohemians	104
Crossing the Blues in March	105
Picnics	106
Out of Dreams I Come to Light	108
Riding Out	109
This Might Be Our Story	110
In Court	112
Moving the Old Stone	113
Admonitions on Turning Sixty-One	114
Freshman Mime: Talent Show, Caldwell, September, 1961	116
Visitor in December	118
A Horse Person Opera	117
Winter Bananas (1974-2016)	120
The Man Who Broke His Crown	121
Winter Dreamer	122
Deal Canyon Birds After the 2017 Blizzard	123

Acknowledgments
About the Author

from *OFF THE MAIN ROAD* (1978)

Fungi and Algae loved each other
but the world was hard, bare, cold–

Fall Dance

Last night the wind
in a short cold storm
blew all the apples down
covered them with snow.
Old Jonathans
pruned last fall
pollenized in spring
watered, thinned
propped with pine poles
I glean them now:
bushels and bushels
of windfalls–dead ripe–
changed in the hand
of weather to cider.
We'll start the press
tomorrow and watch
their juice run into
jugs that save
their lives. I hope
they're sweet. Ah
they are. Next year
vinegar, wine. Ha!

Tomato

How long did you expect to live
out there in the old reality garden,
Tomato? You couldn't grow forever.
We picked you green off dying vines
before the frost could black your face
and now you've made a ripe globe
on brown November's window sills.
We're so hungry for you, Tomato,
our knives flash in our teeth.

Slicing the summer continent open,
we are your conquistadores, Tomato.
Our eyes land gleaming with hope
on your archipelago of seeds.
We discover isthmus after isthmus
of flesh and juice. We're driven
by hurricanes, the need for salt
until our sails finally fall still
in the middle of a strange sea.

The windless acid force drawing us
westward is known to no one on our ship.
We throw our horses overboard mañana.
We know not if we will die here
or on some distant tongue of land
or if we shall ever return to España
The scurvy is not in these latitudes.
Tonight, we pray for wind or rain
and dream of our gardens in *Sevilla*.

Setting Backfire

Such a day
I would walk out
any open door
start over
the Blue Mountains
asking a woman
I didn't know
too well
to come with me
the one in Lawrence's poem
"I Wish I knew..."

Up there, we'd make
each other
a fire at noon
rolling and blowing
the tinder of our skin
spinning the old friction
in our bones to flames
letting them burn
to keep us warm
an hour.

For days, we would
be off
walking wilderness
with our packs
on fire
never looking back
for the cage:
table and bed
full of kissless lips
cold chicken thighs
that leave the living
fed well and dead.
And we will not
return the same.

Our eyelids will be gone
and we'll be smoldering
trying to think
how to contain
the next blind lightning
that burns beyond this line.

Words

This isn't a street
I live on, it's a road
where ditches sing

and that's not timber
on the hills, that's trees
each with an old address

and this isn't lawn
I'm on, it's grass
blooming with lions.

These little differences
would make a world if
I could keep them growing.

Let's see: is it water
or the creek that flows?
Gravel, rock, stone?

Could you hold this for
a while? I'm stumped now.
Be back tomorrow.

Song for Carpenters After Summer

Lay down your hammer's head and claw
muzzle the handsaw teeth
wrap the level's floating eyes
hang up the rusted square
lay the blockplane on its gleaming side
so the blade can rest.
Carpenter, journeyman
the house is done.

Empty your pockets of headless nails
sweep up the sawdust
check the angles cut in June
with your August eye. Are they true?
Will they hold the weight of snow?
Gather the curled shavings in your hands,
carpenter. Wear them.
They are rings from your old wedding
to the trees.

Poem Against the First Grade

Alex, my son, with backberry jam
smeared ear to ear and laughing,
rides his unbroken joy with words
so fast we let him get away
on the jamjar without clean cheeks first.

He spills frasasas
tea with milk and honey;
a red-chafted schlicker
beats our cottonwood drum.
Thumping the pano keys
like a mudpie chef,
he goes wild with words
at the wittle wooden
arms inside, a hundred
Pinoschios to singsong.
If he can't wide byebye
bike to the candy store,
where he is Master Rich
with one penny, words turn
to tears in his mouf. Once
in a while, he walks home
with pum-pum-pumpernickel bread
his nose twitching so fast
a wabbit would love him.

Now this language is not taught in first grade.
Alicia, his tister, knows this fact.
But he juggles it around all day
until she makes him spit it out like
a catseye marble or a tack. "Ax," she says,
"that's not right." She's been among giants
who wipe off the dialect of backberry jam,
then pour hot wax on each bright mistake.

I hope for a bad seal on Ax and tister,
encourage the mold of joyous error
that proper sad giants, armed to the ears
with pencils and rules, all forgot.

Directions for Visitors

If you want to find my place
get out of town any way you can.
Find the Cascades in early morning.
When you see the Tatoosh Peaks
where the Nisqually flows
into Alder Lake at Elbe, stop,
ask directions at the grocery.
I won't be mourning in the tavern.
The Post Office closed last year.
I have no phone and mail hardly comes.

Take the road to Alder by the lake.
When you see the garden above the road
that will be Uncle Ernest's homestead.
He's 95 this year, prays every day.
Keep going. When you reach the crest
you will see Uncle Leonard's pasture
on the left, Grandpa Mayo's honey house
across the road. Grandma still lives
that farm alone. Cross the swamp
on Alder Creek past Uncle Charlie's pond.
My father's house is on the left knoll.
He died and I moved away to town.

On the next wide curve, turn right
onto the gravel going uphill until
you come to a Dead End sign hidden
in the grass and fireweed. Turn there.
To the right. This will be two ruts
a berm of grass down the center
mudpuddles and chuckholes all along.
In one place, a creek flows across.
No more signs now. Curves will be blind.
I'd suggest slowing down.

In two miles, you'll come to a gate.
Park there and get out. You will hear
Clear Creek splashing over stones,
a dipper will welcome you upstream.
Follow the current through bracken
buttercups, devil club, blackberries
skunk cabbage, deadfall cedar and alder
until you come to a waterfall and pool
surrounded by second growth fir.
I should be there fishing somewhere.
You may see the smoke from my fire
rising like a ghost through green limbs.

If you don't see me, don't call.
This place can't hear a shouting voice.
I'll know you have come by the way
the crows and chickadees carry on.
I'll come out then and eat lunch
with you and we can talk and feed sticks
to the fire. If you wait an hour or more
and I don't appear somehow,
I'm simply not the George you knew.

Catch a few fish for yourself then–
under the falls is the best cast.
If my fire's out, there's still wood.
Make a fire of your own, eat, get warm,
and leave the same way you came by dark.
Please do not tell anyone where I live.
Try to forget this place all the way home.

Bird Talk

On one shoulder–magpie.
On the other–red chicken.
As I walk around people
ask, "Do they talk?"
I smile and the birds
put their beaks in my ears
and whisper stereo.
What you hear me say is
only what I've been told
somehow by this wild
black and white thief of
all that gleams and this
creator of brown egg still
warm in my hand. At times
this means a headful of war.

Split Kindling

With my hatchet filed to a feather,
guillotine in that French revolt,
I take a quiet bolt of cedar
by the neck, set it on the block.
This wood is wise; it starts to chant.

Up and split down, up and split down,
my hatchet hand chops steady as a butcher's
cleaver one inch from my thumb
while thin bodies of sticks fall singing
in a crisscross heap.

I cut this old growth from the swamp–
cedar kindling the color of hot flesh,
crux of every revolution in its grain–
for all the cold inward mornings
I need to hear the song in new wood fire.

Forgive Us...

Fifty years of your butchering art
are here, Grandfather. I hear the crash
of your falling ax into alder, the whisk
of your keen knife on the blue steel
while lambs and wethers bleat in the barn.

They know your one quick stroke across
their throats would make their ends
the best you could create. I still don't
like the blood, Grandfather, but I know
now the need for meat.

"Nothing should suffer," you said,
and sought out old dying queens in hives
and pinched their heads. Mensik's calf–
you told us not to watch; bad dreams
would come, you said, so we walked out

and watched you anyway through a crack
in the wall–one sudden deadly swing
from the spiking maul buckled the calf
instantly to its knees on the hay.
We knew your power then, and ran away.

And now this God, Grandfather, this God
whose songs you sang, whose church
your worship built, whose book you read,
whose name you never said in vain–
He's got you here in his shepherd's barn.

Oh, he's a shoddy butcher, Grandfather.
He's making you suffer his rusty dull
deathknife for years, crippling your legs,
then cutting off your speech to tremble,
then tying you up in a manured bed.
He won't bring you down with any grace
or skill or swift humane strike of steel.

Day after day, you sit in His hallway
in your wheelchair and nurses walk by
like angels and shout half your name.

Ah, this God of yours, Grandfather, this
God has not learned even the most simple
lesson from the country of your hands.
You should have taught him how to hone
His knife, that the slaughtering of rams
is the work of those brave enough to love
a fast deft end.

Inviting Alex to the Bees

You want to come along?
I'm going down to hive the swarm
on the fence this afternoon.
Yes, you might get stung
but I'll try to show you old
Grandpa's way among the bees.
His smoker's lit–if you'd like
to hold and squeeze the bellows
steady while I tie this knot
in the strings of your veil,
the knot he tied for me.
You ready now? Let's go.
How do beekeepers live? Oh,
slowly with the smoke
nothing fast or harsh or dark,
wearing white, standing away
from flight, working the spring
days alone in acres of bloom.
Hear the honeyflow? That hum?
Easy. Let me take your hand.
There's the queen. Still, now.
Let's try to get her in.
By fall, she'll have her house
also chuckablock with light.

Report on Grandparents' House

They die, they go off gray
their closets hung with clothes
empty as blue cellar jars.

Their kitchen seems to shrink
when you walk in. That spider
whispers at his feast of moth

by the rusted drain and weevils
eat the Gold Medal off the flour.
When you sit down, ghosts boil

up in motes of a living room.
Buck horns and Jesus nailed
on the pine wall want to speak

while mallards fly from
their frame into the plaque
of Proverbs across the room.

None of this is yours by law.
Blood owns it all, owns you.
Can you let it go?

How to Live Two Days in Osburn, Idaho

Dredge, the Welshman, drunk again
wants to hear a steel-driving song,
says get down to yourself and sing.
"Don't stop now–both feet in the air."
You have to play for him.

The seedling in the yard grows in
a cage. Protection is the school.
By the greenhouse, girls dance on a fence,
laughing at the mud chuckholed street.
You have to play for them.

At the Emerald Empire Motel, a woman sweeps.
She knows the room's not much,
but the sheets are clean. You can use her
phone for local calls, that's all.
You play up to her.

The miner watches his son pick grounders
on the dirt diamond. He talks big fights,
smokes his pipe inside his pickup cab.
They're all hard-hit liners here. To know,
just play third a while.

The lions at the Lion's Club don't roar
without another drink bought loudly by
the local editor, named Penny, who's
got a copper head that's a company ante.
You play hob with them, not poker.

The girls in Wallace at the Lux will
ask you to their rooms. They thought you'd
left their Coeur d'Alene the day those
kids ran Ballet Folk out of town.
You play fast and loose with them.
The woman from Burke who's eighty-two
says she's the only one left alive

in her family. She brings down a diary,
wants to salvage her own brief history.
Play straight with her.

Your teeth ache, remember the mines
a mile deep. Sunshine's not a friend here,
and Bunker Hill's a war. These men dig all
the silver, and they are always poor.
At work, you ply these words for them,

for anyone patching scraps and fog together
between a year of strikes and bad weather,
for anyone planting tomatoes by the slag heap
by the river running clean again this year.
Just make this play for them all.

Be the two-day singer in this town.
Wait for them to come for coffee in the cafe;
listen carefully and stare up the canyon.
When they go, write this in the streets
and play fair, by god, with every voice you hear.

Off the Main Road

Wandering with your wife
down the highway in rain to
keep the rust off your feet,

the matches in your pack see
a farmhouse. "Is this the place
I want to be?" you ask yourself.

"What will I be going blind to
if I stay here seven years?"
Your hands lead you inside

to a cold stove. You lay a fire
full of answers that tell you "Stay."
Soon, you have hung a door, a sash,

stacked wood, tilled the garden,
fed the white chickens, sat inside
mornings reading the rain falling.

On that farm off the main road
bluebirds bring you the exact daze
of spring. In June, you see dolphins

in delphinium blooming, trade toad-
stools for mushrooms, those gray birds
for towhees, finches, wrens. Millions

of frantic sperm that made your past
will–in one place–create surprise
that changes everything–your eyes born

again. So unpack. Nothing's lost
by stopping: everywhere begins where
you dead end. Just move in and in.

from **MARKING THE MAGIC CIRCLE**
(1987)

                no flowers, people, fruit, or trees, no
                dirt where roots could hide and feed.

Early Morning: Washington 12 toward Ohanapecosh

Along the dammed Cowlitz River
stump ranch fields are thickening
with swampgrass and buttercups.
Blackberries are always overgrowing
cedar stumps jutting like monuments
in the pasture. Alders jump the fence
ferns move in, moss takes the shake roof
and swallows fly out the kitchen window
over mole hills and rank thistles.

I could be farming that homestead
long enough to see my own posts rot
my fences rust and disappear in floods.
I was born to this land; land is my name.
Here means my first father died, my uncles
aunts and cousins live, my brother and I played
summers away in grandfather's timothy and clover.
I know the faller's ax, pulaski, froe,
peavey, scythe, the crosscut saw.

Davis Creek, Tilton River,
Rainy Valley, Packwood, Mossyrock–
the small loggerheaded towns asleep
in the century of their own sawdust
the logging trucks aiming their reaches
like howitzers at the silent Cascades.
Sawlogs wait prisoner at the mill;
teepee burner glows like rusted hell.
Bare bulb of the yard light burns over
the yellow crummy streaked with dew.

I could be a gyppo sleeping in that shack
where the junked-out cars are full of dust.
I could be swinging out of bed on hoot owl
caulks and hard hat my only human hope.
I could be pulling green chain at the mill
packing a black lunchbucket, driving home

half-drunk from the Ashford Tavern payday.
I've chased chokers, borne off cants,
slung tongs, stickered and stacked on bunks
until I didn't know who my own hands were.

As sun burns around the corner
I give this valley all the names I have
drive myself for higher country on Rainier–
Indian Bar, Summerland, Mystic Lake–
the alpine park no man will ever cut
where I'll camp tonight and sleep
a glacial sleep for lives I'll always be.

When I come down, no one in these towns
will know my name or consider the avalanche
of lupine melting in my hands like laws.
I'll see the second growth and death of work
then fly like a shining crow for the river.

My Mother Is This White Wind Cleaning

out. Everything. From Grandma's house.
Laos is a refugee. Laos needs a place.
Laos is sponsored by her church–
those singing fundamentalists.

Out old clothes. Out thirty years of dirt.
Nothing's to be left.
Salvation's Army marches here–
converting love to modest rent.

Oh she has reasons heaped holy
on a silver platter, theological as
the head of John the Baptist.
Order, too. There's a box to Dump

there's a box for Goodwill, a box to Burn.
I'm reeling from them all.
I stay away and help. Late at night,
she asks me what I'll want to take.

"Save me Grandma's diaries, the morning
in June she called me outside to see
the salamander slide under the door,
odor of geraniums in the air.

Save me that place I slept and dreamed
for thirty years," I say.
She writhes. Gold rings twist themselves
around her fingers. She's down to blurt:

"All this must be done. Your aunt
and I are just sick of these decisions."
I nod. I know it is too late to teach
her to leave the soul of just one

earthly home alone or call it love's
unvendible estate. She knows not where
she comes from or where she goes.
She is borne again by her far God—

the cleansing homeless storm. I'm still
her son, the troublemaker. Here, growing,
a tree bent again by all her prevailing.
Where next, oh righteous tornado?

High Cascades

love pacific rain, curve
wind, bear old storms, explode,
turn ice to glacier lily bloom.
Hear that first tick of melting

snow? Meadow blue with awe?
Hear springs seep, creeks clatter,
white water roar, falls pour
wet thunder, mist, rainbow

spray? Oh range so fragile, dangerous
your beauty washes every face
your flow redeems the stone. Thirsty
for the true, we take you in.

Larch in Fall

All my life I've seen you slowly going gold
slowly letting go your shade another year
felt your needles ticking down your limbs
to soothe the summer duff to sleep again–
your soft voice falling in October light.

Your gold tongue is spotfire on the ridge
saying silently that change must come where all
those changeless conifers believe that any turn
from official hue can mean the end, and still
you flare and freeze on steep north slopes.

In Idaho, you asked what color I would be.
I stared at you, said subtle green, said gold,
brown, black wet, and living in Montana
you gave me fence and roof and beams, and here
your form still gives me shape in cavities of snag.

You stand now as ghost women on the mountain whose
blood is sinking in my veins at night
whose double names I take to like confounding hope
whose heartwood is the tough straight muscle that
gives me light, whose fire is fire that speaks as

it burns up. I chose you, Larch, to all those
splattering loud leaves in hard and famous forests
in some country far from this interior, this west.
Hold to that ridge for me another year, hold to
that brilliance mottling the falling light

so still and clear–my changer who remains.

The Black Wolf of Love

This landowner thinks he's rich
but weeds lord all his ground.
They carry me–cheat and foxtail–
over his broken stile.

In the fallow field, I hear
the property belongs to banks.
The tenant farmer's dog comes out
then stalks my tracks.

This pasture's owned by Widow Jean
whose perfect yard I mark.
Her grass I call a Mushroom Town.
For mayor, I nominate the moon.

Across the road, I walk the freehold
of the Church. They built
this fort for God's Indian trade.
The factor calls me Skulk.

Over another fence, I'm on open land
owned by creeks and meadowlarks,
hawks and wind. Each sound is a deed.
Their courthouse is my ear.

Vaulting the chain link fence,
I fall into the library of death.
The grass is mowed. Plastics flinch
by the stone books holding breath

as I pass. Now seventh is the state.
The field's open, tilted, green.
Harvest here is balls and bats
and children's screams.

I steal my shadow over this trail.
Trespass is my name.
I am the black wolf of love.
Nothing is mine. I just go around,

A Gallon of Honey in Glass

Here–a sweet stone
to ride your shelf
a lost summer
given shape to last.

Here–what keeps
guarded by stinging.
This is your voice
whispering "Home."

Here, the perfect
field is flowing
against the bitter
that winter brings.

The specks of wax
will hope to feel
your slowly stare.
Savor such light

as your tongue can say.
Thousands and thousands
of shimmering lives
have brought you love.

Here is proof.
Dip in your hands.

Conjuring a Basque Ghost

for Jean Ospital(1930-1979)

You died as I could–
snag on the mind. I've fallen enough
timber to know how easy it is not to hear
that slight deadly crack in the top.
I know you didn't look up. The chainsaw roared
in your ears as you stood waiting like
a lamb while the widowmaker fell.

Three white horses graze your pasture now,
Jean Ospital. Your gates are locked, wife gone
to town, boys back in school two weeks after
the funeral. All your sheep are gone in steel
trucks. At your auction, everything sold high.
The realtor is out there now nailing up For Sale.

Do you want me to show how you loved your dogs
or drank the brown goat's milk? Should I say we
spoke in *Espano*l that day going down to buy
those five black fleeces still waiting here?
Should I say the ache in your eyes as you saw
the pasture dying in the heat, your ewes

grown thin? Should I put here your jeans
reeked with lanolin and sweat? Should I buy
your farm? I had no such money when the empty
trucks rolled in. What do you want from me?

Watching my wife spin the wool your dead hands
sheared, I make this prayer for you, Jean Ospital:
Pyrenees, receive this man. I send him home.
Inside the mountain that watched him being born,
cover him with wool and let him dream.
This is all I can say for you. *Adios, pastor.*
Leave me now. I have wood to cut today.

Report from East of the Mountains

Don't say much.
This close to Hell's Canyon
the rimrocks want quiet

so Nez Perce dead can sleep.
Your mouth is dust all August
when the barn roof shines

so steep you must look away.
This is the vast interior now
where fallow ground mumbles

"Leave us alone." So be empty
enough to wonder into ponderosa
wild enough to kiss Narcissa

Whitman's ghost wavering across
swales and flats of wheat.
The populous wet coast?

You won't see that trench again.
Alkali and sage hens take you
basalt remakes your fencing hands,

your eyes trace magpies on
rivers of east wind. So be remote.
Visitors may never see this

lost range you settled for–
juniper, mule deer, Appaloosa,
buckaroo, riata, Chinese gold.

One Umatilla is your friend.
High blue day on high blue day
the hidden spring gives up its

cold artesian calm. This water
keeps you close to shade, to bones.
By ravenous deserted towns

you are small as a gnat's ear.
At night by an obsidian sky
singing surrounds you—

deep, fragile, far. With such edges
you can let the center go.
The world starts here and is whole.

Coyote Teaches Jesus a New Word

They were going along the Blue Mountains in deep snow. Jesus kept falling through the crust up to his waist, but Coyote was singing and dancing along the top. Jesus was getting mad at Coyote, so he said: "I'll bet you can't even melt this snow." So Coyote said: "Watch. I will do it." He thought a word and the snow melted. Then he laughed and ran up the ridge onto the snow again, leaving Jesus to flounder in the drifts.

All morning, Jesus tried to get Coyote to say that magic word out loud. Coyote got tired and said, "O.K., I'll teach you the word if you promise not to say it too much." Jesus promised. So Old Man Coyote taught Jesus the Indian word *CHINOOK*. "As many times as you say it, snow will melt in a warm wind that many days, but never say it more than three times," Coyote said.

Jesus laughed. "CHINOOK, CHINOOK, CHINOOK, CHINOOK," he said, took another breath and said, "CHINOOK, CHINOOK, CHINOOK," and he kept laughing and saying it over and over. Pretty soon, the creeks started to roar, the rivers overflowed, the valleys flooded. Jesus was so happy he had learned a new word that wasn't in the Bible. He was going crazy.

Pretty soon, Jesus started to melt too. His white robe and skin melted right into the ground. Coyote looked around for him a while, but there wasn't even a bone left. "Oh well, I warned him," Coyote said. "How did I know he would go too far?"

This is why there are so many bad floods now in the spring. This is why they had to make two hundred dams on the Columbia River. White people all over the low country know Jesus is up there in those mountains again. They know he is saying "CHINOOK, CHINOOK, CHINOOK" but they can't make him stop. All they can say is "Jesus" or "Jesus Christ" when the high water comes.

Professors in Their Masks as Fence Posts

Nothing holds us together
but staples and tension
some stiff chunks of alphabet
at the corners.

Our job is acting afraid
to make exceptions, even
for the shadow of that bull
who might need range.

Split up, shrunk, stuck
in high-paid holes, we wear
old moss caps, pay our dues
to the prevailing weather

and hope the dream deer
will come again tonight
and go easily over
this taut barbaric wire.

Blue Hour: Grandview Cemetery

Three miles out, I die down in grass
guessing here I might be alone enough
to lie and stare an hour. Home is far.
Beside me, black Sancho dog holds his breath
then runs off–cocked after something

articulate with the possibilities of night.
Six ridges away, I hear wildfire burns
driven by hot wind, fought by 800 men.
Today, I watched boys with .22s
killing gophers, as I once did, for fun.

Across the valley, smoke is towering
like a god from fields of grass
burning for the sake of purity, they say.
Why am I so cool and easy now? Still,
alone, cradling my head in my hands

considering evenly
the scream of killdeer over fallow ground
my own yellowjacket sting
the millionaire next door
my jilted neighbor who gave herself away
Venus brighter above the ridge,
I remember the sign at the gate:
NO LOITERING, GUNS, OR ANIMALS ALLOWED.

So let them arrest me. Come on, sheriff.
Find me if you can. I'm guilty, I know,
I must be guilty of too much peace
too many inviolate hours just lying
on my back in the grass out of town.

I whistle through my teeth. I laugh.
I wait. Here comes that old black shepherd
stinking of skunk to break me out of
this bony wilderness of graves where
for an hour, I was modern, criminal, free–
stealing space for one more groundless prayer

Sleeping Upstairs

After the kiss, the tucking in
the footsteps down, the light out
always he listens in the night–
a boy alone in his attic bed–
for late cars sizzling by in rain
sees their transient lights washing
on the strong rafters just overhead.
Warm in soft flannel pajamas
warm under Grandma's comforters–
his hand holding onto a bedpost–
he lies awake in the dark.
The sandman comes after prayers.
"If I should die before I wake
I pray the Lord my soul to take,"
was what he had been taught.
What he believes is the sound
of rain on Grandpa's cedar shakes
lulling him, easing him to sleep
the sound of those old voices below
holding him safely there–upstairs.

from ***WEST OF PARADISE***
(1999)

> Some eon they got married, settled
> down. Together, they got the hardest job
> in the world–eating rocks, making dirt.

The Emperor Breeds Only on the Ice

after Robert Ardrey

When March comes, and that southern autumn
darkens into winter, pairs of emperor penguins
march inland across the Antarctic ice
to that place where they must breed.

On fathomless freeze, she lays their single egg
and he picks up the egg on his foot.
Then she and her friends go back to the sea–
their only source of food.

Close among the circle of males,
each with an egg on his foot, he remains.
They begin to move. Perpetual night encloses them.
The zero winter blows, shudders,

snaps, crushes, torments them now
as it has tormented every year.
Each stands with an egg on his foot.
Shoulder to shoulder, they preserve their heat.

There are no fights over property,
dominance, borders, ideologies.
Once, twice, the night clears.
They see the Southern Cross–its crucifixion clear.

The southern aurora displays its veils–
faraway, shifting, impalpable,
tantalizing, rewardless.
More often, the storm whites them out.

Wind cuts cold beyond calculation.
For two months on that fathomless ice,
they live the terror of soft illumination
and they revolve there–

this fasting masculine mass–
each with an egg on his foot
presenting this one on the edge to hostility
giving that one at the center a moment of warmth.

Can we apprehend these nights?
In a mass of male emperor penguins?
Revolving? Each with an egg
on his foot?

In a dark, frozen, endless Antarctic?
Beneath withdrawn stars?
You do not know, I shall not know.
We must learn this kind of love.

Five Six Minutes in March

Morning, that red cockadoodlum, calls me
awake to light alarming the wall.
"Review, retreat," my dreams tell me
as I wait on the pillow. The parade
of naked emperors will pass again–
the children still asleep upstairs.

Opening the quilts, my skin leaps
past the mirror that stares crazy
out the window at apple trunks.
Nothing flinches as I, naked father,
ride the tense balls of my feet
to the fire. I find it in ash.

In the kitchen, I strip a ripe orange
from Modesto, eat it, shivering.
Across the valley, snow announces
the first blue birds. A thin red line
of blood wants to rise past 40 again.
Coffee's a volcano, the honey's local.

Cats cry hungry at the door. I open to
lions and tigers dwarfed and tame. Did
Nebuchadnezzar throw me in this den?
My feet say "socks." I eat chocolate cake.
Who can argue? Interest is higher now
than it's ever been. I tiptoe back

to the bedroom past the hostages held
by the mad mirror. My wife is asleep.
All night, part of her is listening
for the cries of children or lost mice.
At breakfast, she'll translate nine new
smiles for the dog. I grab my glad rags

in a bunch and run for the shaggy rug.
It is a good day for making cedar doors–
louver by louver. So many scraps need to be
put together. Now I've finished this one.
Light comes through the open spaces here
but always indirectly, and I install no
easy latch for closing.

Among Decoys

Two wild geese flying internation
wings came soaring down on slow grace
to rest among what seemed their kind
on a remote pond–wilderness listening around.

Decoys bobbed neat wooden heads and bills
when those geese splashed in. No eyelid
moved. Their random bodies seemed alive,
a refuge, a community at ease, at home.

Perfectly deceived, those two wild birds
let their bilingual billing gabble on
and on, their migratory music be silence
articulate between themselves. They fed on secrets

in the marsh, dove for dreams, loved October
–echoing–and mountains flaring gold fire
around them. When decoys did not answer, those
wild birds began to wonder if the locals

were just polite?–maybe just demure?–
maybe mute?–maybe souls at peace?–
wild geese pinioned each possibility aloud.
As blue, then gray, then no light fell,

the decoys held their painted faces smart.
All night, their perfect wings were still–
their carved silence absolute, invulnerable.
At dawn, as two wild geese rowed softly upward

through late stars, calculating guns began
to fire from public blinds where those
decoy makers concealed their careful aims.
Wild blood turned that pond incarnadine.

The decoys stared their usual fake stares
of perfect, empty, and deceptive selves
and they nodded on and on and on.
They had done their jobs—such good actors—

poseurs all dumb, deaf, mindless, blind—
ideal shapes advertising an illusion—
perfect—for making a killing—

In the Time of Gold Trees

The doe comes down carefully to kale.
In the dark, she come nibbling
so quiet the dog doesn't hear–
thief, lover, dreamer, ghost.
It is late November now–too late
to change–too late–
the kale so green, so rich that
snow cannot touch its potency.
How did she know it was time?

The doe comes down for kale.
In the morning, half the leaves
are gone. Nothing but her perfect
tracks are left for me to taste–
those triangles in my soil
that will never disappear.
How did she know I grew this ripeness here?
How did she discern such vulnerability?
I'm forty eight this fall.

The doe comes down at dark for kale.
I shout. She runs. I think of poaching
her sweet steaks–meat close to home.
"There is a doe eating the kale,"
I tell my wife. "Don't kill her,"
she says. So, she will continue
to take my garden to Glass Mountain.
Half of my row is there now–
half of my life gone–
Why did she come this year? Why now?

Why is she made of fire?

Excuses in Snow

The morning of deep snow I, being lost
as usual after early class, wandered out to study
the white tons fallen overnight–new, silent, absolute.
Breathing in the frozen air as though I were
some explorer staggering toward a pole
living some discovery I had to know, I stood
on icy treacherous steps of stone and stared
as snow plows arranged this storm in berms.
As I waited there, an older student came to me:

"Sorry to be late today. The blind calf came
through our fence again. I had to get her in.
The neighbors were gone. She might have died
if I hadn't stayed." I turned to her–fifty, stocky
bright, fair–she lived a farm far out of town.
"Blind calf? How can this be?" I asked.
"Why they keep her–I don't know," she said
"I put her in the pen with our blind cow."
"Blind cow?" I asked again.
"I don't know why we keep her either."
"Black Angus?" I asked.
"Yes," she said.
"A blind black calf lost in two feet of snow–
how does it find its way?" I asked incredulous.
She stared at me. She didn't know the continent
where I stood–thirty years of teaching gone
my head a private blizzard of its own.
"It must know where feed and water are," she said.
"At your barn?" I asked.
"Yes," she said, "that's where the calf always comes.
What did I miss?" she asked.

"Let's go in," I said and walked with her–hot coffee in
the union waiting, attendance drifting beyond control–
all late too late life excused again–by storm.

A Hanford Veteran: Jay Mullen's Story

From Missouri, we moved to Spirit Lake in 1944.
My father was stationed on Lake Pend Oreille.
He wanted us to be together there.
He wanted to fight to save his family.
He thought we would be safe with him

in Idaho. Then one day when I was five
all my hair just turned white, fell out–
the whole school itching–eyes burning–
we didn't know why. We were kids living
in Idaho where we were safe from war.

It took fifteen years for that radiation
to gather in my throat–my thyroid–here–
he pointed to his neck–and when it did,
I was deathly sick. At 19 and dying
I promised God that if I got over this

I would go anywhere he wanted me. Later, I
went to Africa on a mission for ten years
then came back to Spirit Lake, Idaho, again.
The Presbyterian Church we believed was
still there but lots of things had changed.

My father supported the atom bomb on Japan.
He would have been the first wave
of troops ashore. He was sure we were safe
in Spirit Lake–he would have done anything
to protect us, you know–

and there we were–being destroyed by
the same radiation that was protecting him,
and there we were–in Idaho–of all places–
becoming victims of the same thing
that killed thousands of Japanese

and there we were—sure our parents were
doing everything they could to protect us
but they could not protect us from Hanford's
secret experiments in power. I'm sorry.
I can't tell it without crying now.

On West Burnside, Portland

She tried her thumb against the rip
of traffic that drunk Friday night.
I walked by, sealed against desire,
telling myself I had no car.

Helpless in a block, I turned, went
back, asked if I could, somehow, help.
"See that damn duffel?" she said.
Together, we pulled for a yellow sign.

"At sea, I could save your life,"
she said, "but on land I'm lost."
Scars on scars told more—a flat
dangerous world she sailed.

I left her at the Sea and Land
where she told me, "Tonight, by god,
I won't be no whore." Late, late
in my hotel, loud sirens kept me

waking over and over to sea roar.

Gyppo

Old Joe Padgett ran a lumber mill
sawing Hoodoo pine out Blanchard way.
One Sunday night in Spirit Lake,
our hymns, prayers, testimonies,

my stepfather's preaching–all done
again, Joe held up his right hand.
"See that, boy?" he said to me.
"That taught me patience, so–

let that be a lesson to you now."
In that cold sanctuary, I stared
and stared. His thumb was gone.
Then he shook my hand, his stub

of bone and iron fingers gripped
like God. My face turned red.
I was twelve that year and new
in Idaho. Joe Padgett's voice

burned with wilderness that night
forty years ago. Why can I not
not not forget?

A. J. Dickey Couldn't Run the Ends

bronze October afternoons we played flag
in the park, so he always hiked—our center
until "Statue of Liberty" was called
so he could be a back. He loved that pose,
waiting to fool everyone with fakes
just before his big brown boots began

to cut the turf with his halt steps.
A. J. Dickey couldn't rock those pink-
sweatered nights in gyms of Elvis girls
but he always sang good bass in choir.
Four years we were the back row boys
in jeans, sang blues for school,

Jesus hymns and choruses for God
and holding the last notes of songs,
A. J. would look at me and I at him.
We wondered who would be the first
to breathe. Our voices trembled with vibrato
under flannel shirts and common robes.

A. J. Dickey could not play the floor
or crash the field where good legs ran,
so his blue pen kept every score, his
good hands ran the dying clock
on the gymnasium wall. He hustled
towels, basketballs, and tape, rode

the bus and bench with Coach Butler
every game, came home to frozen midnight
with the team. I still see his careful gait—
short step, short slide, short step—
down Spirit Lake's ice streets.
A. J. had his beat, knew how to fall,

how to heave himself back up.
He knew balance was delicate to keep.
More than once his brother Jim had to
give A. J. his own hands, heart, legs
and arms. We were all the same.
Bright birth flawed us all–somehow.

A. J. was our center–
the first to comprehend.

Segues for Interstate 84, Westbound

Meacham
is married ravens bowing to the roadkill deer. They
peck and waddle through their morning devotions
keeping the immortal circle moving through the sky.
These are the forests where illusions burn.
Eighty years, men fought native fire as enemy
then learned she was their only healing friend and

Spring Creek
is the hill where a woman buried her
new born baby under stones. Her husband cracked
his ox whip and hid behind his mask of beard.
With dirty hands, she wiped her tears.
The dream of settlement smeared the page.
Her ghost is still here–protesting this
hard broken country all set on edge.
Children repair her stream while–year after year–

Holdman
grows a white new-painted sign. Now a formal label
in the field announces "WINTER CANOLA" to everyone.
This is new rape seed flowering yellow for oil.
Someone keeps our language safe and marketable–
as usual–even in the middle of an empty county.
Latin saves us again from thinking definite things like

Pendleton
where big red letters–PG or PGG–ride the plains and
pregnant river hills. The abandoned drive-in
east of town welcomes you, the billboard empty
now of all desire, and Theater Road is weedy
peace. Under bridges, the Umatilla River curves
cold and blue past the dead sawmill. Last year,
the hospital became a prison where chain links
gleam and concertina wire plays a wounded blues:
"Oh baby, nobody escapes from these places,
 baby, nobody gets through two fences" for

60

Rew
where blue pigeons perch on the henhouse ridge
above the elevator. Their work is praying that
this forever wind will not blow their dusty plain
all to hell some day. All directions, wheatland is
naked, standard, private—monoculture built by
markets traded lustily—Tokyo to New York.
When men plow the wind, this dust can kill.
These blue pigeons pray for rain in

Stanfield
where the sign says "HOME OF THE TIGERS" but
only brown tumbleweeds growl and stack silently
against the freeway fence. Over them, one kestrel
winnows the morning median, hunts a minion mouse.
See? Everything wants breakfast and where
is the poet Gerard Manley Hopkins today?
His holy dapple dawn-drawn falcon dives—
here—now at

Boardman
because pylons are profane. These giant skeletons of
steel take the river's power, march off across
the desert for the Willamette, their fists fat with
electricity, their bodies headless, rigid, juiced.
No one dares call them drug lords or pushers or kilowatts
a fix or outlets a local dealer selling pure addiction
to deadly consumption—not yet, not in

Arlington
symbolized by "A." Who remembers the old rivertown
where steamboats used to dock and ferries cross?
The alphabet now arrives in twenty-ton Gray trucks
hauling the steady garbage stream upriver from Portland
and long trains roll down daily—wasted from Seattle.
Here, the first great interior dumping ground that
saves those coastal cities from themselves.
They call it "sanitary" to dignify such lust.
The sign does not say "SEATTLE/PORTLAND LANDFILL—

TONS OF IGNORANCE PER DAY BURIED FOR YOUR
PLEASURE." The "A" on the hill is whitewashed too.
It should be painted red and not like

Woelpern Ranch
this isolate, where white shouts at the gate,
"We're here, we're home, come in, come on."
"NO RETURN TO FREEWAY EASTBOUND" says the sign.
The ridge is a jawbone that opens to the sky.
This basalt watched Joseph ride downriver and
now, industrial wind scatters children far
and another outpost of progress turns marginal
grows doubt, folly, grief, dispossession, fear unlike

The John Day River
lichen who crave these palisades.
There are enough berets of sod
to represent the south of France.
Red and yellow masses paint the cliffs
for miles, and talus slopes arrange
the hard centuries of breakage into
angles of repose. Sometimes, an artist
named Falling Rock gets to the river–
across this easy grade you ride where
lichen crave these palisades beyond

Blaylock Canyon
angling to the water. Now, the rim is Missoula flood?
Ramparts in old wars? Old gods? Nothing fits.
The rhythmic silence of basalt repeats
the rock dove's echo, echo, and echo.
Now, send your smartest Faust. Tell him
to count and name every fissure here in
one square mile of stone; write his report
on infinity–before he dies in

Maryhill
at the museum. Now, no Mary here.
The highway railroad baron–Hill–is dead.

The river turned out not to be the Rhine
and lovers left this mansion for the south.
All night now, chess men by the hundreds
checkmate themselves with subtle moves
as petroglyphs in basement rooms beat drums
and sing for salmon and Klickitat fishermen.
Every morning, the curator must build again
her imported empire of belief around Rodin,
around some Romanian queen's silk gown.
Two red hawks ride the centuries of wind
and paper airplane contests win respect–
beauty institutionalized and this remote
requires any cent or light. Below this art,
sweet Takahashi peaches ripen in

Hood River
sun. Wind changed the water here to cash
when the fish were gone.
Now, butterflies with rich nylon wings
spawn across the espresso river.
Hispanic hands pick your apples,
pears, and cherries by the ton.
Issei leave behind the memory of war
their stolen orchards
the memory of being given
their own fruit to eat while
prisoners on racist relocation trains.
One white mountain still attempts
to be silent and above it all by sending down

Multnomah Falls
sending white water birds diving down
down into the foaming pool.
These never die. Their wings forever
curved with their descending,
they rise, disappear, then
dive down and down again.
and then ascend again anew.

Come clear to me, mountain water
birds, come clear to me again.
I am always listening for
your parallactic cry above

Bonneville
where tons of soft interior wheat slide down the watery
stairway for Asia–noodles for China
by the hundred thousand bushel ride easy–
the barges' white giant letters shouting
"TIDEWATER" and "SHAVER."
Fortunes are made here on the surface while
under water, the spawning chinook circle
and die of hunger. No current carries the odor
of home, no hint of hope to follow.
Here, Woody Guthrie sang his great ironic song
"Roll on Columbia, roll on," while the gates
of dam locked the native river to the treadmill
turbines and their endless civilizing spin.

Fable for an Arrogant Century

Mr. Is wanted to be The Boss.
He tricked his brother, Real Smart,
into killing all the Should Row bums
telling Real his gun shot nothing
but noisy objective blanks.

Real Smart got excited. He and Is
sold a hundred tickets to a lynching
they planned in the woods. Mrs. Hightech
came in her black gown. She sold popcorn
while people watched those outlaws

Maybe-The-Kid and his Uncle Seems
get doused with gasoline. Everybody left.
Mr. Is and Real got rich. Science, Inc.
built them an imperial house of cards.
Miss Universe moved in. They had fun.

Everything was perfect until one night
two Indian kids named Wonders and Doubts
started wiggling their ears and singing
in the street. The whole house suddenly
disappeared in an inexplicable smoke.

A Father Speaks to His Son
the Only Boy in the Seventh Grade Choir

Let me hear you.
You won't always be surrounded by
those forty-seven gigantic girls
wobbling over you on pretending heels.
Forget your sweating hands, your crotch
where jockey shorts insist you scratch.

Let me hear you sing. Lift your chin.
Just think your breath below your waist.
Try not to worry about your hair.
The song is what we came to hear
so give yourself to each note
sustaining that long phrase.

This easy, two-part melody will change
and you won't always be alto, I guarantee,
so be patient with yourself.
Concentrate on the back row. I'm sorry
your mother's at work again tonight.
Don't let that tie and collar choke you.

Whatever tries to keep you from
the sound that is your own–be it school,
parent, team, or town–let them know
you won't be shut up
by any of their champions, big principals,
or degrees of fear. Be a singer, kid.

Let me hear you now. That's good alto.
In a year or two, you'll begin to growl.
There's no disgrace in a changing voice.
You'll be diving then–as you must–
for the bottom of the world.

Voice from Another Wilderness

north of Hadrian's Wall, 128 AD

A long time
we were living old
in the north before the Romans.

We watched them march.
They wanted slaves.
Our fists tightened on our spears.

We strung our bows
with fierce belief
and waited for the dark. Romans are easy

to kill at night.
They cannot see us
painted as we are with clay and ash.

We fight them now
for everything we love–
our deer, our wives, our trees.

They say Romans will never
go home. We can't leave these hills.
Tonight, we attack the garrison and retreat.

Be with us, gods
of the river. Caves
in the mountains, wait for us.

Caractacus, we come.

Family Scavenger

Believes in refuse and loves junk so much
he haunts the household dumps–attic, cellar,
will, hope chest, cobweb closet, gravestone,
leather album with sepia prints, that barrel
of letters in the ditch in rain–Scavenger
seeks the lost family silence at the heart.

Gathering every artifact in sight–snapshots
box by box, bloody letters from the war,
the diaries of years alone, Bibles by the ton,
ivory razor, tusks, pistols, lockets,
clipped curls, albums, lace, sheet music
of the sea–no song too minor–Scavenger packs

them to his cave. Soon he knocks on your life–
jovial as he tells you why your eyes were born,
tells you Emma Goldstein is your definite ancestor
so you're not all goy, tells you who stole
your name, who cut your childish curls, who
put your life inside these stories he has found–

your great uncle falling backward into the goose
pond before he sailed to America to sober up;
that hateful aunt abandoning her little sister
to housekeeping while she enjoyed a pious year
at midwest Bible school; your carpenter grandfather
kicked out of the church he built; your uncle

crippled for life when a school teacher jilted
him, eloped with her student lover to California;
your Scots grandfather a Grenadier in bearskin hat
guarding the bier of Queen Victoria all night;
crossing America in boxcars come your pious aunts;
grandmother comes a child through Ellis Island gates;

your dead cousins pose with their cougar hounds;
your German ancestors chop undercuts into trees
so huge that trees became their enemies to burn,
and cedar was the only gold they knew for years.
When Scavenger leaves, your room reeks the salt
sweet sweat memory of love and ghost and give.

You can never be alone in America again.
The silent lost lives in your bones have come
to sound. Your mouth begins to sing some song
you do not know, some pent crude music
you cannot understand but always hear, some five
piece ensemble beating in your ear.

The Treehouse at 316 North Regent Street, Burlington, Washington

for my brother Douglas

Remember that great English walnut tree
curving over us, huge shelter in soft green
shade? Remember our treehouse there–that
refuge two boys built of third-grade scraps?

New stepsons then of Rev. Venn, we plied
and played those old boards into a roof
that didn't leak in rain. We munched sardines
and crackers there, prattled our Pig Latin

on the tincan telephone. Remember? You taught
me how to climb up: stand on the garbage can,
raise both hands, lock them tight around
the first branch, then hanging upside down,

throw one leg over the limb and swing yourself
upright. Our treehouse was too high for adult
righteousness to reach–we kept silence about that–
and we sat too quietly to be caught reading

those banned and sinful comic books–
Superman, Batman, Bugs Bunny, Red Ryder–
secret gifts from our kick-the-can friends
like Frankie Younger, Dave Wollen, Ida June.

Remember how those taboo pages stained
our fingers? We would hide those pulpy heroes
in our secret place–the damp tree crotch
under the floor–just above the reach of

that hardwood stick with which new
Stepfather beat our hands red with pain
if we did not eat every bite of liver or
corn soup by the time he set on the clock.

Remember that stiff self-righteous stick?
Remember the grief of meals in that manse?
In our walnut tree, we ate without fear,
read for hours—brothers together—

boyish infidels hiding from the blind
crusader of an angry God. You, my brother,
came down and became devout on Saturdays—
like him in your way. Part of me is still

up there—where these English leaves still
shelter me from zealotry I learned to fear.

My Aunt, Helen of Avon

Sickly, small, premature,
a goatsmilk baby, hard to suckle,
she couldn't see to read. Every day
school and home were trouble.

Her mother shunned her while
her beautiful, talented sister
won scholarships to walk on water.
Her father, her only friend,

took her for long afternoons
in the "Model A" as he sold
his fireweed honey door to door
up the Puyallup Depression valley.

There was only one day of joy
she could remember. At school,
Aunt Helen won a sewing contest
in the seventh grade.

Fifty years later, she still knew
her first and only prize–
touring the new dam in Alder–
the hot odor of electricity spinning.

After that, Prince Charming turned
out to be a drunken logger she
met at church. Three sons died
childless and young. The fourth

ran as far as time would let him.
Her days came true in junk mail, clutter,
housework (she always hated), rain, TV,
wood fires, tall grass, dark rooms,

and driving her Avon route in stump
country where she could tell her best
soap, perfume, and powder customers
her story over coffee–and they loved her.
You can keep your lady from Troy.

Uncle Leonard, Penitent

for my cousin, Carl Falck (1948-1966)

After her son was shipped to Portland–
a grenade fragment from Vietnam–
Aunt Helen remembered Carl had said
there was no place for him to sleep
in the house when he came home–tired
from basic in his neat fatigues.

So after cutting Weyerhaeuser timber
all day in his black wool underwear,
each night–taking up his pick, shovel,
and wheelbarrow–Uncle Leonard attacked
the dirt under his house to carve out
the new basement.

For a year Uncle Leonard dug, dug
faithfully, counted carefully each
shovelful he threw–55,000–
he would say–exactly 55,000
shovelfuls of dirt, and that count
gave him some incessant ache–

some countless pain beyond his back.
Eventually, the Army sent medals, ribbons,
$5,000 for his son's life. That was all most
welcome, countable, and spent quickly
for blocks, concrete, mortar, curtains,
whitewash, and carpet in the rooms.

The monument was done. You could sleep
there underground–inside this penance,
this room made of guilt, booze, and doom.
Soon, Bible class was meeting there again–
taught by Leonard, the missionary's son.

Sometime, you should visit this known
soldier's tomb in Washington–the state,
that is–yes, where Rainier guards the gloom.
You can't see it from the road but I know
the way to those descending stairs and–

Elegy for a Migratory Beekeeper

for George L. Mayo 1894-1980

Ah, Grandfather, bring one last load of honey home.
Let it be wild clover from Moses Coulee or Palouse
a mountain range away. Let us hear you shift and slow
down the rolling summer tons, the blue homing truck,

that Chevrolet. I will call, "He's back," and run to open
the pasture gate. Let Grandma phone the Rathie girls to come
to work next week. Let me swing wide those honey house
doors again, wrestle my big brother on the sticky

floor. Ah, bring one last load of honey home, Grandfather.
We'll untie your knots, coil the hemp ropes as you yawn,
slide arthritic from the truck–beat at sixty five from
hours of crossing Snoqualmie, your bees three hundred miles

away. We'd sing "Tipperary" and "Irish Eyes" to keep awake,
remember? All night, I fed you mints, salt nuts by the sack,
Black Jack by the stick. Remember that time in Entiat?
The truckstop waitress there? We sang "Danny Boy" to her

for pie. Give us that sweet weight again, Grandfather.
We'll pry the covers off your last load and hear the hum
of that lost bee–the one who forgot to leave the comb.
She stowed away inside her cell, stung me between the eyes

to almost tears. You're that bee now, Grandfather. You're
that cell. You're buried in the valley now, and I'm still
here remembering you, Alder, that honey house, your wisdom,
art, abundance forever. Ah, give us those white-combed fat

supers to carry in again–weight to stagger boys into men.
Fire the boiler. Let my brother Doug clean the wax melter.
Sweet steam will warm our extracting room. Blonde Alice will
wield the hot uncapping knife opening these cells to

gleam. Ah, Grandfather, bring us one last load of honey home. As we whirl in this extracting world, let those summers—when you taught us how to live—crystalize and come to rest here now. My eyes are swollen shut, Grandfather,

and memory folds my hands for the strong old singer—gone.

Grandma Wilhelmina at Eighty-Five

I'm alone here now with cats
my windows overgrown.
I knit afghans day on day
and death waits in my room.

I've lived too long.
My Father's gone for years.
My words are slow
as moss on stone.

When my daughter comes
to check on me
I'm going to say,
"Let's get the garden in."

I've lived too many years
by this lake shore soft
above the Alder Dam–the fishing
getting worse, they say.

Nothing now I have to do.
I read and sleep and knit
grow my fingernails
more brittle, my hair green.

See my gallons of buttons
saved? My desk cluttered
with clipped obituaries
and old cards? Nothing ever

thrown away. My children live
nearby. I see my grandchildren
every day. They bring me mail,
paper, food, and company.

All my life, I believed in
Jesus and taught my little
Sunday School class at
Alder church to love the Lord.

Please tell me, tell me
one more time–
what was my maiden name back home?

Where was I born?
How long has my Andy been gone?

Star

in memory of William Stafford (1914-1993)

Maybe every night a star wakes up
leaves your house and climbs
into the sky to be itself
among the galaxies of prayer.

Maybe when the sun is gold again
that star returns to sleep
somewhere inside your doors–
some blind spot you can never see.

Maybe this creature is with you
there–somehow–say as a mother
spider God made, her web so delicate
we're all caught–shimmering.

Eternity is here sleeping–somewhere–
common and silent. When you dream no one
is looking, eternity escapes again–
subtle, quiet, awake–consumed by light.

Be like that star.

The Lichen Family Story

Fungi and Algae loved each other
but the world was hard, bare, cold–
no flowers, people, fruit, or trees, no
dirt where roots could hide and feed.

Some eon they got married, settled
down. Together, they got the hardest job
in the world–eating rocks, making dirt.
For a 120 million years of work, Fungi

and Algae stuck together, never quit.
Their fragile quiet relatives spread out.
Can you see this pair? Their furious old
feast? Your life–a Lichen lovers' gift?

June Night, Full Moon

Past midnight I wake alone.
Moonlight comes–lover–to me now.
Windows wide, her luminous body

moves over my bed with soft strong
arms I sense but never feel come on.
Heaving off my sheets, I open, turn,

give all my naked dreaming life away.
She laves me with her voice, dark eyes.
Her tongue rouses me with sad cosmic

joy–a man untouched by any hands–
human or divine–two solitary years.
She illuminates me with orgasmic still

silver light, then clouds away. Alone
again, falling through the illusion of her
limbs, I cannot sleep–so full of avatar–

lips rich with the salt taste of her skin,
with how she–fearless with delight–
came over me–nightlight incarnate–

showed me the whole soul, body, mind
her sky all magnificent beyond me still.
Dreamer, oh dreamer, come again, again.

Eagle Cap

The mountain in Mirror Lake does not waver
in the wind. This means Wallowa calm has come.

Even tons of stone have settled down for a few
million years of sleep. From mistletoe and fir,

shade lulls your eyes. From deep water, your
new face rises slow. Some old grief sinks away.

Water Music, The Upper Imnaha River

The old voice of the rain turned our
clear creeks into one silver river that
afternoon. We wandered upstream together
hand in hand through the Twin Lakes burn—
that forest of black dead standing trees
listening to our slow footsteps fall.

Sun came along. We studied white snags,
with black branches, black snags with
white branches, stopped, kissed, went
slowly on, stopped, kissed again.
Over fallen needles of the trail, we saw
pine trunks torn by bears for food, firs

carved with cavities for new homes.
You named rudbeckia, larkspur—lives
so close and new I could not tell them
from my own. You named the downy tapping,
seeking sustenance on the burned lodgepole.
Where a clear creek chattered on beside

a purple giant boulder and black snag,
I put red ripe thimbleberry on your tongue.
You found an small orange moth, showed
me wings, laid them in the dust again.
Under those black dead standing trees,
fireweed multiplied its graceful redpink

phoenix plumes. Wildfire—destroyer, creator—
made this beauty germinate, flower, fill
with nectar now. Wild bees hummed
through that understory of sweet bloom.
We understood. We too have been through terror
burned, fought, refused to die, regenerated with

roots in memory too fine for words.
Crossing the wilderness boundary,
one sudden hummingbird streaked up
perched its green iridescent wings, one
chambered beating heart in the center
of that forest of dead trees. We heard

the river flowing over stones. You said
the light on riffles was the same as light
that gleamed on the black cracked snags
stripped dead and clean–cubed columns
of charcoal spires sixty feet in the air.
We marveled there, held our easy way

together all that afternoon, joined by
that world we found–alive, magnificent,
old fire flowering among dead trees.
All that old burnt heartwood, we knew,
must fall finally down to feed the wild
lives who come to flourish now.

We were strong enough that day to
listen without divisions, our separate
selves moving together the way tanagers
fly. Eating apples at the Blue Hole,
we saw love's silver water gather, flow,
blend, swirl, cut through stone forever.

A Dream of Two

In her dark kitchen,
a woman sits at peace on her floor
looking at a man she loves. He
sits before her there. They are naked now
but do not touch. They do not speak.
Each is empty of all fear, all desire.
They seem to be trees living by some
underground river quietly flowing
out of each other.

In the space between them,
a heap of bright leaves gleams
as though soft diamond light flowed
like huge water up from underground.
They do not know where those burning
leaves have come from or where they go
or how that light came to flow mysterious
unconsumed between them there.

In their shared stillness,
the woman studies his shadow, seems
to add another leaf, then the man does
the same. Nothing they can do
seems to change
the light from the leaves
the shadows playing over
them. There is so much
they cannot understand

so much peace between
them there–they do not want
to, cannot move.

from **PUBLISHED UNCOLLECTED POEMS**
(2000–)

For a 120 million years of work, Fungi
and Algae stuck together, never quit.
Their fragile quiet relatives spread out.

In the Cabinet Shop, You Never Know...

At the bandsaw cutting out two
perfect maple circles, Orville,
my friend the cabinetmaker, said,
"Once, I cut out the world for

a mission talk at church"–and
he formed the round of earth with
ten good fingers on his hands.
"Remember that tabletop you

cut out for me?" I asked.
"That was years ago," he said,
"and the table is still round."
We went to the drill press then

to sink the holes for dowels.
The bit smoked and scorched
drilled the hard rock maple stock.
"Feel that," Orville said, handed

me the circle and his newest hole.
Heat covered my middle finger.
"Just like my second date," he said
straight-faced, as I cracked up.

"I married a virgin, you know."
"No," I said, "I hadn't heard."
"My kids laugh when I tell them.
They still don't believe me," he said

and put those double rings of maple
in my hands–good work done with
good will again. I never knew what
Orville might say next like,

"Seen my board stretcher anywhere?"
or, holding up his crafty hands, said,
"A bandsaw, my friend, likes to eat
Butterfingers. Watch out."

Awakening

All night, while you sleep, one
green tree just beyond your pane
plashes and bows and trembles

in the rain, trying not to break
in wind that never could relent.
This morning, you look out–

the wind has died, rain stopped.
One green gold life, one form,
one tree stands obvious enough.

Bold limbs begin to celebrate,
to transform light, to sweetly feed
that fine tenacious mass of roots–

fists that gripped the earth last night–
so blind, dark, invisible, below
too deep in our underworld to see.

May all the holy furious roots you
hold keep you live and green, awake
to love and give in any storm.

Blue Mountain March

Brown water braids and foams
swirls among the flooded willows
as their gold limbs bud and sway.

The slough runs bank to bank
again–full with all-night rain as
grass and sage begin to green.

On the high ridge, a herd of deer
in gray coats and white tails safely
graze the sweet greening spring.

Magpies gleam in hawthorn nests,
red-winged blackbirds chunk-a-ree
from tules all across the marsh.

One new black calf trots across
the mud feed lot to bump her mother's
milky bag and suck pink teats again.

Red Hawk wheels above the barn,
shops for her first gopher.
Nothing moves in the wet field.

One young bull sniffs, lifts his
chin on the heifer's back, rears up,
mounts, dismounts, subsides.

Across the valley, clouds of snow
tower and billow and fall against
mountains of blue pine and sky.

Green fields of winter wheat begin
to love. When longing light comes,
ripeness is all– our seed, our grain, our end.

Crawl Space

Tight dirt underworld–that's where
many men must live. Crawling on their guts,
breathing dank, no room to sit, they drag

their tools and drop lights under some old house–
broken pipes, sewage, muck, ants,
bad wires, termites, dry rot, uneven

joist, bad floor, broken heat–and all of that
they fix and fix in that tight flat silent hole
where widow spiders, rats, snakes, cat shit,

skunks, disease, broken glass all wait.
Fine dust fills their lungs with shorter life,
their nostrils plug. Cobwebs fill their eyes while

just above their faces–certain heels march
unaware of how many men must live
righting spaces there are very few to love.

Easter on "B" Avenue with Doe and Fawns

Come to the window now. See? There she is–
Mrs. White Throat, the bold doe I named last
year for that unorthodox patch beneath her chin.
In spring, she comes down from the crucified

mountains to my back yard–again–to feast
on quince blossoms and immortal willow.
Don't move. Out the window, you can see
her black eyes gleam as she bites each

sweet and newborn leaf between her teeth.
See there? Her twin fawns? They're still as
grave stones in the shade of old mock orange.
Mrs. White Throat suckles them, hides them

while she feeds–though their spots are gone.
See how she has not yet shed her gray coat
of hollow winter hair ? See her white rump
patch, her short gray black-tipped tail flick?

See how her grace lifts one back leg to scratch
behind her ear with her delicate black hoof?
Oh. Now she's full and lying her long body
down in deeper grass. Time to ruminate again

each sweet discovery of this redemptive world.
See her jaw work? Her cheek bulge with cud?
See her soft silk ears rotate side to side for
dangerous sounds–cougar, coyote, human, god?

An unchurched doe with fawns–is this enough
resurrection for today? Is quince arising from
the grave enough eternity to praise? Let us turn
to the window and stare and pray–wide-eyed–
for all that dies and loves and comes again.

*Street Cries, Spain**

Salamanca, 1965

Up the still dark stairs
where you hover at the last edge of sleep
his bass voice comes chanting
the first holy fact of a Salamanca day:

    El Pan-a-der-o—
    El Pan-a-der-o—

three low notes, then two high.
You hear the door latch click.
Senora Teodora Sanchez descends
for her round loaves of morning bread.

Pushing his blue handcart and grindstone
down the siesta street, he rolls on
steel wheels singing his passing presence
to all the closed, white-washed doors:

    El A-fi-la-dor—
    El A-fi-la-dor—

rising, falling, rising–his low tenor sure–
his knives sharp enough to kill.
No one comes out. Children of Valencia
follow him–taunting his monkey.

Alicante. From labyrinthine streets, from
whitewashed walls, his voice seems to
be the silence of olives groves and Moors
in an old Mediterranean afternoon:

    El Si-llero—
    El Si-llero—

one tenor call every three minutes–no more–
high, low, middle–his tune forever
resolving softly with his wood wheelbarrow:
there must be chairs to mend by the sea.

The blind man with his bad goiter
hunkers against the sandstone pillar
in the plaza–his white cane tapping
the frozen flagstones–lottery tickets pinned

to his overcoat like daily medallions.
His baritone call resonates across
the frozen classical Castilian afternoon:

>   *La Lo-te-ri-a—*
>   *La Lo-te-ri-a Para Hoy—*
>   *Toca El Gordo—*
>   *La Loteria—*

Twenty-five years ago–hitchhiker, student–
I heard these cries in the streets of Spain.
Franco was dying. I had only money for food.
These nameless voices called out to me then–

ineffable courage, indelible music.
I cannot forget them, I cannot.
They carry me along–even now–toward hope
that someone is listening within–

to a singer passing–
to a singer bringing some necessity along.

---

*
Note: the italicized Spanish is sung.

The Engineer in Love at Fifty-Five

Rolling along easy and steady
under that soft gold summer moon
riding the solid bed of ballast, ties, rails
engine following the route he knows
the tonnage of his coupled freight
confidently traveling the luminous night

The Engineer suddenly sees ahead
the rails disappearing into water–
those clear parallel lines he trusts–
gone to shimmering black and silver
riffles moving shadows everywhere.
"Slow down," The Engineer tells

himself, "This water in moonlight is
not deep"–though he has no way to
prove that. Denial is always his first guess.
Maybe Lost Creek just over flowed
somehow, a short crest, a rise from
some summer burst of storm.

Then The Engineer begins to wonder.
Washout is a chance, derailment, death.
Maybe he should yank the air brake
set the squeal of steel on steel
bring the hurtling cars of his life's
night freight to a halt.

What should he do? He cannot turn.
The moon is thick with shadow now.
He hesitates. Doubt pours over him.
Momentum chooses the way as
bright water opens and explodes. His loco-
motive launches a wide wake of

of soft black-silver waves. His heart
lurches in his throat, carries him down
watery tracks into a world he does not
know. Moon the color of fool's gold
lights his way. Going down, he hears
a woman crying out his name.

Spring Work

In these old greening hills
a human fire burns. I cut out

deadwood, lop off suckers of
new sap, take down heart rot,

disease, breakage, crisscrossed
ramification. All these I heap up

feed to flame and dance in smoke
as they burn down to this glow

of orange coals and gray ash–
altar of a day. I did not come

here to live forever, but for
one more year, this is my

signal fire to you so far away:
I am still here among old trees–

keeper of what lives and dies.

Teacher in the Desert

Pour out your life as water on dry ground,
then, when you think you're empty
pour out your life again.

Watch yourself slowly soak away and disappear
without–you think–the slightest trace
that you poured your life

out like water here. Face it: you may now sing
or you could moan. Whatever springs
from this life you gave for love

you may never see come green. The seeds of earth
lie all potential, and lives unknown
might someday grow from your

lost years–your wordless bones. So, today, once more,
take the longer view. Pour out your life
as water on dry ground

then, when you think you're empty
pour out your life again.

The World According to Apples

Two thousand green apples hang on the tree,
enough to break its branches down.
I thin a thousand one May afternoon
to save the tree and bring my harvest home.

June nights, silent gray moths mate
in the limbs, then codling females flutter
blossom to blossom in the dark, lay
their tiny eggs in nearly every fruit.

One July afternoon, huge anvil clouds
arise, white hailstones thunder down,
shredding leaves, bruising half the fruit,
bringing down what can't hold on.

August days, the red squirrels walk
the tightrope telephone lines, scamper
through the tree, nibble, taste the green
skins, let fall the sour on their tongues.

September and color coming on, blue
jay, starling, flicker, magpie fill the red
fruit with birdpecks everywhere–
a free feast they keep up for weeks.

October. Windfalls red in dying grass.
I leave them there for the doe and her
twin fawns sneaking down the mountain
every night, eating every apple up.

Today, I pick the remnant fruit, cut out
bruises, birdpecks, worms, cook one batch
of butter, make one pie to eat, one poem
to make it sweet–a la mode.

My harvest mostly lost, the tree, at least, is whole.
One more year, I gave my life away to hunger.
All winter I will see these apples I let go
fly and feed and pray around me in the snow.

from **NEW AND UNPUBLISHED POEMS**
(2000–)

Can you see this pair? Their furious old
feast? Your life–a Lichen lovers' gift?

Inside the Foreign Experts' Compound

for Ai Qing, Changsha, 1982

Rain empties on Hunan–
January, a gray afternoon.
The grind of steel skates
across the wall is gone.

I go to the gatekeeper's wife
to ask her for some fire.
My family 10,000 miles gone.
No letters in three weeks.

From this blue concrete room
I see one peasant working alone
in his garden. His heavy hoe
falls and rises silently

among his winter vegetables–
his hat a mountain in Oregon
across the Pacific Ocean.
I must boil more water now

translate years of silent exile
onto these icy Chinese walls
as steaming tea warms my
cold and solo and alien fingers.

After Divorce

Such grief has come to you before,
so sleep with every window open
now. Embrace night's old galaxies

and wake to fiery sky again.
Feast on honey grain gone gold
and study the remembering floor–

dust is all yours now to design–
and welcome old November wind–
those same spiders at your door.

Let some close poseurs withdraw.
They needed to disappear
like endless news of the newest

deadly mass catastrophe.
Retreat from madmen who explode
in smithereens for some idea.

Tell the years of blood sacrifice
not to expect your lambs again.
Say only now what must be said–

name and sort and name and sort
these lives you can and cannot live,
then dive and lave your solo selves

in blue pools of rivers under words.
Memorize one silent mountain tree
that ash–so live and leafless there–

orange ripe clustered naked fruit –
all still–all hanging fire–

.

Waiting for the Bohemians

Standing in January slush and thaw
Under an old mountain ash
orange clusters of berries dangle there–
mythic tree with heavy limbs ablaze–
thousands of sweet fires against the azure
afternoon. Ah, more succulence your lips
can't take in. So stare, be still, then
wonder–how long before bohemian wings
remember this good tree, fall down the sky,
feast here again? Oh wild banditti, my lovers
of orange, ferment, seed, skin, aura, root,
stem, all this winter ripeness hangs naked fire–
here–for you. Where is your hunger feeding now?

Crossing the Blues in March

How many nights now have you climbed
these switchbacks up the wild Blues?
What waits for you at Deadman's Pass–
black ice, fog, snow, sleet, hail, freezing rain–
no way to know. Jackknifed trucks, cars
piled up, spun out, rolled, totaled out–
these mountains breed sudden wreckage.
You could die, here, tonight.

A few flakes fall lazy on Interstate 84.
By the reservation line spring blizzard hits.
No plows yet. Beyond your feeble lights,
breaking up and up, endless lines of snow
flow over you and mesmerize your eyes.
You're trapped in some whiteout tunnel.
You can't see ahead or back. Shining mile
posts are all that guide you here. Visibility
zeros down. You shift to 4-wheel, hope no
one has stopped, no truck spun out, no
snowplow sudden in your face.

How long you drive like that you can
not tell. Time disappears. White lines
break around you, hypnotize your life.
Years come and go. A snowy number 241
suddenly shines briefly and is gone.
Unbroken skeins of white flow on–
as though you're buried in whitewater
and can not come up. Speed is nothing now.

Images of the curves come back to you.
You see the roadbed on a summer day
and follow that picture in the storm.
Your steady engine hums along. Some
Portland jazz you've never heard before
beats drums from far away. By Spring
Creek, imagination wins. Once more,
you live to tell the time you did not die
that night on Cabbage Hill.

Picnics

By the river we sat down to eat together.
June evening cooled the cottonwoods
as gold light played silver shadows across
the riffle. We sat close to each

other at our table by the river.
Your hands tossed our salad to gourmet–
potato, asparagus, mushroom, red pepper–
the dressing was your hot peanut

Thai at that table by the river.
Cold salmon was pink, firm, and slippery
when we kissed each other and drank
cold sweet water, our cups running

over on our table by the river.
Slicing the olive bread, you said, "Sometime,
we should make love outdoors."
Your silly spaniel waded in the shallows

close to our table by the river.
Finished eating, we held our hands
crossed the old gray concrete bridge
together, walked away–sated–

left our table by the river
to follow ruts of ox and pioneer.
You showed me "Cats Ears," a native
tribe still living in the wild grass

far from our table by the river.
There, I did not tell you of that good
woman who I did not seduce here
though she asked me to, or that

frightened woman who loathed any touch
if we ever sat at any table by any river.
How long did we wander, kiss, and stare?
How long can we be those two hungry lovers—

their picnic over, their table empty?
No river. I can't tell you now.

Out of Dreams I Come to Light

All night, I sang Bach again to strangers
passing down some crowded corridor.

One stranger recognized St. Matthew's
"Break forth, oh beauteous heavenly light

and usher in the morning...." He called
to me, I called to him, "Idaho, 1963."

He smiled, disappeared. Who was that face,
that voice from choirs thirty years ago?

Those naked days I robed my life in black
and gold, sang oratorios beyond belief–

gave every breath to my great conductor–
Thomas. His flowing hands, his shadow

wings led me to the flowering tree where
I wake to thank him now, to hum alone

my new solo morning song again.

Riding Out

Cycling wheels roll easy down the black road this afternoon.
Your legs rise and fall. Spokes gleam. May sun obscures
itself behind some clouds, then appears in gold again.
Vast grass mountains, high pine forests rise before you now.
Endless green. Your chain turns. Magpies row across the wind,
hawks pray the sky. One squirrel holds last year's black walnut
in her teeth–bitter shell, sweet core. On her post, she watches you.

May wind is gently fair. Beside the road, ten grazing mares–
foals at every side. You see new lives trembling along–all legs–their
mothers' teats never far away. Further on, the black bull–
huge in his corral– waits for hay from hands he knows by smell.
A mile up the hill, a red heifer–white horned, serene–turns to stare
as you ascend the afternoon. In a far field, one old ponderosa stands
alone–left in the middle of that green plain to signify the

way the world portends. Your heart's drum beats louder now
the uphill ride tests everything you are. Flowering crabs flare
crimson in a yard. Dwarf delicious flower by the pond. Huge
haystacks–sere in their austere squares–cast geometric doubts
across the road as you pass through their shadow land. You're
rolling uphill now–going as far as you can–to wherever this road
ends. Green meadows bloom with goddesses who lave and dazzle

stones, gods melting to the sea as you ascend, sprockets gleaming in
the shifting afternoon, your eyes your arms already flying through
the pines. "Come to us, come now," the green trees say with open
limbs. "Come. Let go of all desire. Life is grief and pain. You
understand. So let go, let this valley go. We are waiting here for
you. Be one of us again. Eternity is now– mysterious
and whole–and you are cycling toward us again today. Stay on
this road. You will rise, curve, disappear–singing–into fog. ..."

This Might Be Our Story

for retiring EOU faculty, 2002

From lives far away we all came here
moved by hope and hunger and half empty U-Haul vans.
Sophisticate and green, riding the golden clouds of our degrees,
we came down to this college in the wilderness–
settlers dreaming, anxious, fertile, driven, new.

Nothing turned out as it seemed. Shock after comedown shock–
we were isolate, small, remote. The place was wind and cold,
the town ugly, press illiterate, people narrow, racist, poor,
our classes huge, pay low, library so small it hurt, bad puns
everywhere, the crazy roller coaster budget of the state.

In that outpost, we started to teach, create, hike, write,
walk, drive, travel, orbit, run, ski, cycle, withdraw, fight–
any way to resist, revise, repulse the nowhere life in hell.
At least, our wives said, our children could grow up safely here.
Schools weren't too bad. We found houses to fix and furnish,

trees, vines, flowers, and shrubs to plant, gardens to feed us–
if we loved enough to water, weed, and reap. Around us,
green mountains flowered. Year by year, small changes came–
promotion, merit, sabbatical, new colleague, leave, friend.
Against all petty tyrannies we asserted our own equations, arts,

routines, disciplines, moves–the run at noon, nights of reading,
summer seminars, fellowships of far and near, discoveries of
both true and false from urban jungles passing through. Then,
some fall forgotten now, peace came along–opened our
blind eyes to gold mountain light. Eventually, we could love

that impossible class, arrogant colleague, dull text, even tolerate
committees, memoranda tons, ignore administrative jerks.
What opened you up? Was it that turquoise river carrying you
all afternoon, that one student who understood, that idyllic place
you knew was worse, antique tree giving apples year on year?

Slowly, our outpost became *refugium*, our old homes retreat,
winters beauty, valley peace, university mature, the state budget
a carousel of legislative asses. Beneath Athena's mask of stone
even the town and press and populace seem–some days–to pull
their heads out of the empire of sawdust, beef, and greed.

Now we are going far again and who knows where?
Hope and hunger move us still. Students now attending each new
day, we wear the silver badge of courage here–graduates beyond
degrees of fear. We leave to you this universe within the
wilderness and wander on–grateful, veteran, dreaming, anxious,
fertile, driven, new.

In Court

Ms. Too Many Cats sways back and forth
presents her 300 pounds, her huge blonde
wig, her red rouge cheeks before the judge.
Impassive as the sphinx of Egypt long ago,
she blinks, waits, stares, and sways while
the animal control officers–athletic women
neat in short hair, uniforms, and belts–point out
her neighbors have complained for years that

her house reeks urine, cat scat fills every room
her toms roam, snarl, breed and fight all night,
litters of kittens pour out in numberless dozens.
As Ms. Too Many Cats stares down the starry flag,
they testify she's too poor to feed them all.
They testify she doesn't get them fixed.
No one can go in her house without a mask.
In his black choir robe, the grave judge sits, decides:

"No cats for five years," he says, "'and tomorrow
 you must give up all your kittens at 11 00 a.m.
Is that a convenient time" he asks–polite as wind.
Swaying, her red lipstick in a clownish frown,
Ms. Too Many Cats cups her hand behind her ear
stares at the judge, sways in her old sand coat
She's deaf–this citizen. She stands there heavy,
lonely, desolate–a woman gone wild. As the gavel

falls on her debility, Ms. Too Many Cats is silent now.
When the bailiff leads her out to pay her fine,
a kitten–black/white–suddenly pops out her collar,
stares around, lets out one plaintive long and loud
"meeooowww." The gallery, where I sit with my son,
explodes in joy. The judge, pharaoh of all sentences,
remains monumentally demure, pyramidal,
composing the gold mask of his dying face again.

Moving the Old Stone

One gray stone sits beneath the oak—
oval, huge, alone, larger than any single
man could lift, heavier than sin.

All afternoon, you size up that monster
bring out your steel bar for lever
load three box elder fulcrum blocks

in your old two-wheeled garden cart.
Inch by inch, you pry up that stone
until it stands on end, then with one

great heave, you roll that monster
in the cart and curse its shape with
some triumphant groan—or worse.

When you grip the handle, start to roll
that stone away, those old cart wheels
squeal and groan. The weight

seems more than you can pull.
Your heart begins to pound, your sweat
to pour. To move one stone—uphill

alone—is almost more than any
single man can do alone. You go by
inches then. You hear some metal tear.

That old cart seems loaded with despair.
At the rock garden, thirty years away,
you dump that stone and see it fall

into place and stay—all gray again.
As you put your tools and that cart away
rain turns that August stone to gleam.

Admonitions on Turning Sixty-One

Free light awakens you again
plays through the turning leaves
that die into their golden selves
perfected in their fall. Your bed
is warm. You linger there, watch
the bars of Blue Mountain sunrise
take your bachelor bed. Why rush?
You won't be sixty one again.

Old slippers and white Turkish robe
wait on the chair. That black walnut
lamp your brother turned some forty
years ago in Idaho rises–solid, round–
from your Grandma Mayo's birch
side table. You throw back the quilt,
shiver, stand. October shrinks your
naked skin. OK. Let your knees creak.

Breakfast is late. You make biscuits
to honor your grandfather, wash four
purple windfall plums, peel a dented
apple from your tree, cut out the worm
rot at the core. In the glass French press,
black coffee steeps. Honey drips from
your spoon. Let the frozen blackberry jam
stain your tongue, forgive your sins.

On the phone, your brother and his wife
sing "Happy Birthday" from 100 miles
west. From LA, your mother says her card
will be late this year. From Portland,
your son wants to send a washer/dryer.
"Not that you're a dirty old man," he jokes,
and from Redmond, let your daughter–
like her mother–stamp and mail more silence.
Opening your blind, a tabby cat stares in
–white vest, gray stripes, four white feet.
She's one of those nine lives that hunt
your vacant lot, the best mousing around

the neighborhood. Beyond the pussy willow,
your fallow garden lies rich and littered with
a summer's weeds tilled under. Above it all,
you can let go the mountains of blue sky.

On line, the woman at the bank explains
why their web site kept you out. Last month–
–first time in your life–you overdrew, forgot
how to count. It's good she can't see your half-bald
silver head. You might seem poorer than you are–
old explorer in some wild country on a coin.
When your numbers crunch, they start to hurt.
So, your health costs a fortune now. So what?

Sitting down to write, past Octobers smolder–
days you shook the ripe trees of Burlington and
sweet plums rained down, days you rode your bike
–no hands–slammed the Seattle news on the sleeping
 porches of Bellingham, days you threw touchdowns,
shot Idaho's fat deer, loved Sharon, Alice, Kathy, Jean,
wandered Spain, tasted sweet sex, got pregnant first,
then married. All those fires–let the ashes glow.

Now–a new grandfather never ready to be old–
go into your next life. This afternoon, your new friend
will take you to a lake above this town where you will
launch two kayaks on wide and shimmering water.
Drifting along together, we will name the wild birds–
bufflehead, kingfisher, hawk, grebe, coot–then come
home by dark to dinner. Through dangers, toils, and snares
you've already come. Get smart. Let go of this October.
You can't be sixty and this ignorant forever.

Freshman Mime: Talent Show, Caldwell, September, 1961

In memory of Anna Marie Walton Boles (1942-2015)

Alone, she walks to center stage, flood lights rise,
she waits, poised, motionless until the music starts:
blue bib overalls, one naked shoulder– strap undone,
cuffs ripped, barefoot, yellow straw hat, grass in her hand–
all elbows and knees and hips moving in rhythm–I stare
spellbound at my dancing classmate, an Idaho bumpkin:

> *They say don't go on Wolverton Mountain*
> *If you're looking for a wife*
> *'Cause Clifton Clowers has a pretty young daughter*
> *He's mighty handy with a gun and a knife*
>
> *Her tender lips are sweeter than honey*
> *And Wolverton Mountain protects her there*
> *The bears and the birds tell Clifton Clowers*
> *If a stranger should enter there*

The program gives her name, Anna Marie Walton, Hansen.
She climbs love's invisible mountain. Hands shaping hips,
she becomes the pretty young daughter among the bears
and flowers, her honey lips ripe for the ascending lover.

Who would reach her? Who would brave the killer father,
befriend the bears and flowers? Taste those honey lips?
That unforgettable afternoon I first saw her dance–acting
out, articulating the lonesome brave lover in us all–

I didn't know my friend Texas Jan Boles was riding north.
Four years later, he climbed Wolverton, dispensed Clowers
and one secret weekend those two eloped to Nevada, got
hitched, and came home dripping honey, skin, and flowers.

A Horse Person Opera

Pacing his mud corral, chewing
down half-rotten rails, old stud
watches night and day for
his rider to come home.

She throws him a flake as
she drives back and forth–
so busy, so happy at work
with new lady friends–

that old husband horse can
wait. He has his water
barn, stall, salt, old hay.
Habitually she doesn't stop

never touches his name.
She owns him–free and clear.
She knows he is alone, but
a cut-proud horse learns to

wait–so her mother taught.
One night, he breaks the rot
runs off with a flaming mare.
The rider cries and cries

when he first disappears
then righteousness saves her.
After all, her stud has left her
she is not to blame–

and she still owns him–
that damn buckin' hayburner
she's kept around for years–
the old bastard anyway–

Visitor in December

At midnight, you watch the shadowy doe
jump your fence–pickets buried in new snow.
She knows exactly what she's hungry for–
apples that fell all fall underneath my tree–
oh God

she remembers how sweet how full how
many windfall nights fell down for her
and here she comes in cold December
to her memory of feast– buried now, lost
underneath

the feet of furious snow. Still, she stands
there on your shoveled walk, raises her
svelte muzzle in the freezing night, inhales
deep for any source to feed her wildest
hunger now.

Her black nostrils flare and fill with strange
delight. Some new sweet scent descends.
She lifts her shadowy head, inhales again.
Yes, she thinks, above me, vulnerable,
there is food

and she stretches out her strong neck,
her silk and huge and tender radar ears
taking in the night, stretches up,
rears up on her sweet haunches
there and yes

as her chin enters your new-hung bird
feeder dangling from the tree, sweet seeds
spill onto the snow, sweet seeds
stick to her quick wet tongue
so fine

and you, tense, see her invent this dance
she must–lift on two feet, fill her mouth,
come down on four, chew, swallow, then
lift up again–a wild two-step
until every

seed is spilled and gone and you are lost
in laughter and relief and joy as she
jumps your fence and wanders off again.
Jesus, oh Jesus, how little you
can understand.

Winter Bananas (1974-2016)

for the trees on South 18th, La Grande

Passing my old house at the soft edge of town
I saw the gold windfall apples abandoned in
the grass, waiting for October deer to feast.

Twenty four years I loved those old trees–
pruned, watered, thinned. Winter keepers,
their ripeness gave sweet energy and peace.

The house was empty now, my ex-wife
gone to Arizona tennis for the winter, so
I parked my bike, studied the fallen beauty.

Around me there, quiet stubble fields dun,
burnished sun, gossamer gleam, blue dome.
Eighteen years since she turned her back,

said, "Change your expectations or move on."
Such sweet winter fruit. Who would ever care?
No close neighbors to see me open the gate.

I stole in, knelt, picked up three golden
windfalls from my old trees, rode off–
a joyful wild grieving thief–love's apple cart

empty, all my husbandry and trespass–gone.
Here I give them all to you–sweet flesh, bitter
cores, irreconcilable black seeds, decades

of ripeness on that ridge I once called home.

The Man Who Broke His Crown

Why–married young–did Jack sense he owed
Jill some huge debt–a blood red inky deficit?

Why–children born–did Jack sense he'd signed
a double mortgage he never could pay down?

Why–children grown and gone–did Jack sense
some bank lord sold his life out from under him?

Why–the night they burned his home loan–why
did Jack leave Jill clear title to thirty hard years of

work? Tell me why–in the black–did Jack run
and run from closings and contracts–any kind?

Winter Dreamer

In my dream last night, I lie
face down on the floor at the base
of a bamboo wall. There are buildings,
ramadas, heat, shade, endless afternoon.

From that room, I hear the voices
of people looking for me. I am
hiding from them—I don't know
why. My arms cover my neck.

Outstretched, I hear many doors
open and close. Someone gives orders
to find me. Lying there, I do not know
what I have done or why or where.

Then, I feel you appear—as though
only you know how to find me
hiding alone below the bamboo wall.
I do not hear or see you cross

that room but suddenly you cover me
completely. Your warm body presses
against me and we—together—begin to
change slowly into one soft and gleaming

light below the bamboo wall—
free as winter stars on fire.

Deal Canyon Birds After the 2017 Blizzard

for Linda Garcia and Brock Evans

When nothing moves under tons of
white indifference, wild Christmas birds
lure you out to admire their black eyes.
There
a chatter of high starlings wheel, turn,
then descend the frozen blue, settle
their jazz in the naked birch next door.
There
a Steller's jay lands atop the chain
link fence, cocks a black and wily
topknot, struts, then scolds the snow.
There
dark Oregon juncos come down the drifts
flit along the wall and walk, sign their
solos with tiny toes–all filigree in snow.
There
low over the gable, dark winter hawk
hunts, English sparrow in one talon–
lunch on the fly when God looks away.
There
a gobble of turkeys march up the street
leave their trail of triangles for peace
then disappear in mountainous green pines.
There
among the blue spruce limbs, one magpie
lights, balances that baton of lonesome
beautiful tail, black eyes always watching–
There
those gray Asian doves. Their sudden
flights invade the bright hungry afternoon
calling more love, more love, more love–

Acknowledgments

Poems Reprinted from Magazines/Books:
I want to thank editors and publishers of the following media in which poems from *Off the Main Road*, *Marking the Magic Circle*, and *West of Paradise* first appeared in print: *Willow Springs, Oregon East, The Observer, College Composition and Communication, Poetry Texas, Slackwater Review, Pacific Northwest Forum, Hyperion, Poetry Northwest, CutBank, Northwest Review, Ice River, Pacific Northwest Forum, Yipe, Salal Series, Gleanings in Bee Culture, Exhibition, Clearwater Journal, The Kerf, Oregon English, Talking River Review, Hubbub, KSOR Guide to the Arts, Jefferson Monthly*. I also want to thank those editors and publishers who have published poems not yet collected: *Eastern Oregon Review Quarterly, Oregon English Journal, Windfall, The Clymb Magazine*, et al.

Poems Reprinted from Anthologies:
Ten Oregon Poets: Oregon Arts Commission (1975)
Fourteen Oregon Poets: Prescott St. Press (1976)
Pushcart Prize: Best of the Small Presses (1979)
Rain In the Forest, Light In the Trees. (1983)
Idaho's Poetry: A Centennial Anthology (1988)
From Here We Speak: An Anthology of Oregon Poetry (1993)
Prescott St. Reader (1995)
Idaho Handbook (1997)
Portland Lights: A Poetry Anthology (1999)
This Should Be Enough: Second Skagit River Poetry Festival (2002)
Teaching with Fire: Poetry that Sustains the Courage to Teach (2003)
Deer Drink the Moon: Poems of Oregon (2007)
Winged: New Writing on Bees (2014)

Poems on Posters: Poetry in Motion, Poetry Society of America "Eagle Cap" from *West of Paradise*. 2001. (Calligraphed on 12" x 28" and displayed on all Portland busses and trains, 2002.

Poems in Feature Films: "Directions For Visitors" reading from *Off The Main Road* in "Tamanawis Illahee," a feature film by Ron Finne, 1982. Oregon Humanities showings statewide.

Poems in Public Installations: "High Cascades" and "The Lichen Family Story" from *West of Paradise* carved in stone at Cascade Crest Pavilion. New Oregon Zoo, Portland, 1998.

Poems Set to Music:
"Star" from *West of Paradise* and "Report from East of the Mountains" from *Marking the Magic Circle*. Music by John McKinnon. *Songs of Interior Oregon*. Premier 4/15/06

"Directions for Visitors" from *Off the Main Road*. Music by John McKinnon. Premier Eastern Oregon University, 6/5/94;

"Setting Backfire." from *Off The Main Road*. Music by Benjamin Tomassetti. Premier 7 May 1993, Eastern Oregon University touring choir;

"Songs of the Grande Ronde: A Cantata." Music by James Eversole. Five poems from *Off The Main Road*. Premier 23 May 1979 by Eastern Oregon University choir.

On Line:
website: www.georgevenn.com
"George Venn." www.oregonpoeticvoices.org.
Melissa Dalton, ed. Lewis and Clark College, 8/25/11.

Listings/Grants/Awards
Lifetime Achievement Award, The College of Idaho, 2017
West of Paradise: Oregon State Library & *Poetry Northwest:*
    150 Oregon Poetry Books, 10 September 2009
Marking the Magic Circle: "Literary Oregon: 100 Books,
    1800-2000," OCHC/Oregon State Library, 2005
"Poem Against the First Grade, *Teaching with Fire, 2003*
Silver Anniversary Award, EO Regional Arts Council,2002
Distinguished Teaching Award, EO Univesity, 2002
West of Paradise: Oregon Book Award Finalist in Poetry, 2000
"The Emperor Breeds Only on the Ice:" Andres Berger Award
    in Poetry, Northwest Writers, Inc., 1995
Oregon Literature Series: Exemplary Programs Grant,
    National Endowment for the Arts, 1994
Stewart Holbrook Award: OILA, !994
Marking the Magic Circle: Oregon Book Award, Oregon
    Institute of Literary Arts, 1988
"Forgive Us...:" *Pushcart Prize in Poetry,* Pushcart Press, 1980
Breadloaf Writer's Conference. Waiter's Fellowship, 1970

Stephani Stephenson Photo

About the Author

George Venn, Poet, writer, literary historian, editor, linguist, and educator, George Venn (1943) is an eclectic, complex, and distinguished figure in western American literature. As one university press editor described him, "Venn's blend of creativity and scholarship is unique...." His distinguished and eclectic literary practice may be best affirmed by *Marking the Magic Circle* (OSU Press, 1987), a 200-page collection of fiction, poetry, essays, translations, and photographs. In 1988, this book won an Oregon Book Award and silver medal from Literary Arts; in 2005, Oregon Cultural Heritage Commission and the Oregon State Library selected it as one of the 100 best Oregon books in two centuries. As a student, George Venn studied at The College of Idaho, at Central University, Quito, at University of Salamanca, at City Literary Institute, London, and at the University of Montana (MFA 1970). In the 1970s, he won a Breadloaf scholarship and studied briefly with the novelist John Williams. In 1980, his poem "Forgive Us..." from *Off the Main Road* (1978) won a Pushcart Prize. When he received the 1995 Andres Berger Award for Poetry, *The Oregonian* described him as "One of the best-known and most respected poets in the state." His 1999 collection *West of Paradise* (1999) was a finalist for an Oregon Book Award. In 2009, Oregon State Library & *Poetry Northwest* selected *West of Paradise* for their honorific listing "150 Oregon Poetry Books." His poems and prose have been published in regional periodicals and anthologized in seventeen different state, regional, and national collections, most recently in *Teaching with Fire: Poetry that Sustains the Courage to Teach.* His work has been included in the national Poetry in Motion program, carved in stone at the New Oregon Zoo, and featured in the Ron Finne film "Tamanawis Illahee." Three different composers have set his lyrics to music for concert performances across the Pacific Northwest.

His most recent book, *Beaver's Fire* (Red Bat Books, 2016), gathers a selection of non-fiction by and about Pacific Northwest writers 1970-2010.

Made in the USA
Columbia, SC
23 August 2017